PROBLEMATICS

Bart Scott

Berkana Publications
Sebastopol, CA

ISBN: 979-8-9923023-7-0
Published by:
   Berkana Publications
   Sebastopol CA 95472 USA

Author's contact information: *bartscottpoetry@sonic.net*

Cover image: Lorna Ho

Printed in the United States of America

for
the two Wendells

"Listen to the melody."
—Leon Russell

Table of Contents

WTC

He falls headfirst from the mighty tower,
His arms by his side, his eyes open,
Like one of Galileo's spheres. His life
Is consumed by the gravity of the moment,
At thirty-two feet per second per second.

He would like to tell his daughter
That the Italian was entirely correct:
Two objects will fall at the same speed
Regardless of the weight of the soul.

To My Pregnant Wife

It is clear you contain the world.
Not like nesting dolls,
merely the same form repeated
over and over
until nothing remains.

You are richer, more varied:
Each of your cells contains a universe
replete with affirmations
and contradictions,
the whole human mess.
You contain within yourself
the greatest power in the world,
utterly devoid of control.

Did you imagine this transformation
when you took my hand
and enthralled me with your eyes?
Did your kisses anticipate
that from mere impulse
you would create a universe?
When we lay there by the fire
did you contemplate
that the accident of love
would lead to a chaos of affirmation?
Not a change of life,
but its inception.

On the hillside of fecund summer
the milkweed pods have grown
thick, gravid with novelty.
As a wind blows from the west,

you and the weed sway together,
mirroring each other's fullness.
Is there a beauty more fraught
than this? You and the plant,
full to the bursting.

Time the Imperator

It is my morning walk around the neighborhood.
On the slight incline
my heart labors, resentful.
My legs are still functional,
but they convey their complaints,
gentle shooting pains
to remind me I might
have treated them better.

It was not always thus.
A mere four decades ago,
straddling that bicycle with skinny tires,
I challenged the sharp grade of the Marshall Wall,
my heart shouting its commands,
my legs churning with the challenge,
the ecstasy of honest sweat.
The end of the ride was almost post-coital:
a release and calm,
a recognition of the animal core
of my body.

Across the parking lot
a couple walks, hand in hand.
They must be high school sweethearts.
He, trim with a shaggy mop of hair;
her beauty as natural as a lilac.
The engines of their bodies
fire with full corpuscles.
I wish them long lives
that they may look back
to the translucent past
while they strain to reach
their shoelaces.

My Life as a Serial Killer

for Les Bernstein

Perhaps it started with an errant rock,
One I threw with the confidence
That if I could never place a ball
In the catcher's mitt,
I would cause no harm.
By some cosmic accident,
It struck the squirrel on the head.
My first memorial, his body
Tossed over the chain-link fence
Into the vacant lot next door.
The sweetness of remorse.

Afterwards, it was merely waiting.
There was my father, the passing
That left me bereft and aching.
Pain defines us and then
Becomes a habit.
Next, my grandmother,
The benediction of her smile
As she died.

Those griefs, twenty years apart,
Defined a part of me:
The nobility of pain.

As for the rest, time angrily clicks
Its calculations on the abacus of life.
I deserve no credit, I merely
Pore over the spreadsheet of loss.
The brilliant and mad saxophonist
And flat track racer, drowning

continued on next page

His pain in wine and barbiturates;
The physician manque,
Balanced between bourbon
And immobility, and early extinguished.
Over time, the hits keep coming.
The two big men, their size
The measure of their generosity,
Proving that the most robust carriage
Will eventually wear out.
The woman whose intellect shone
Like the filament of an incandescent bulb,
Which then burned out,
Reduced to nonsequiturs and fantasies
Before wasting away.
The ghost of my adolescence,
Fighting fires on the Oregon coast
Until she, too, was consumed.
The street musician whose reach
Surpassed his grasp, and who,
Always playing to his own beat,
One day declined to wake.

Old friends and old lovers
Fading into the dying of the light
Against our futile rage.

What are these to me?
If life is survival, and survival is grief,
I will celebrate the accident
Of my continued presence.
It's a tip of the hat
To transience.
I raise my glass and tune my guitar;

The songs are a keening
And a recognition
I remain despite all odds.
As an observer, my involvement is trivial.
I am merely the clerk for time,
The inexorable accountant of life

Returning Favors

On Sunday morning I bathe my mother.
I am returning the favor, I guess,
Many years after the fact.
She is over 100 now.
The body that entranced two husbands
And bore five children
Is not what it used to be.
She could outdrive men on the golf course,
Her back straight and limber;
Now it is bent and stiff.
Into her 90s, in tennis togs,
Rising on the balls of her feet,
She had a mean serve
That was impossible to return.
She now shuffles, slowed by age.

Her mind is still robust, and
She resents the loss of control
Over her corporeal form.
I steady her in the shower:
Another fall could be catastrophic.
For her, this body is an imposition,
The indignity of living with need.
If she is frail now, no matter.
This woman taught me
Through force of character
That women are not ornaments
And that words have substance.

An image from decades ago:
It is evening. At my mother's house,
Exhausted from a day at work,

I fall asleep on her couch.
Later she tells me: I look at you,
As you are in the moment:
Unshaven, rumpled, unhappy;
But I see you in your entirety,
From the cutting of the cord
Through your impetuous adolescence
To your surprising transition to adulthood.

Is that, then, what happens?
Our lives are written on our bodies,
And our bodies write our lives.
It's not a short story; instead
It's a Dickensian epic or *Gilgamesh*.
It's a history of hope, joy, and loss
Embedded with human contradictions.
The hieroglyphics of her wrinkles
Speak of tenderness and passion,
Vulnerability and resilience,
Secret caresses and searing pain.
As she pushes her walker
She is still the 18-year-old woman
Who, having fallen asleep in the library
On a copy of Milton's *Areopagitica*,
Awoke to the impeccable smile
And compelling grey eyes
Of the man who became my father.

Corduroy

It is corduroy, the thread of the king.
The hallmark of college professors,
Expounding on Milton while drinking
The only lousy sherry they can afford.
A fine accessory for a black turtleneck,
Adorning the arm that punctuates a howl
With the insistent glow of a Camel
Chased with red wine from a jug.
Professor and beatnik: my avatars.
Why do they only drink cheap wine?

It may have nothing to do with royalty.
Duroy is a cloth made in England,
They say, and not the stuff
Of courtiers in plumed hats.
Indeed, it always looks rumpled,
And it appears more at home
At a formica counter than
Among crystal chandeliers.
Etymology lies.

When my father died I had it
Tailored to fit me; I was thin then.
It's now snug on my shoulders.
I rarely wear it; I'm always rumpled,
And this distinctive cloth is redundant.
It was different back then.
Unconscious of style and fashion,
He wore what my mother commanded.
Corduroy was the in thing,
And he wore it like royalty,
Draping his arm across my shoulder,
Telling me I would be all right,

While the wales of the cloth
Bore down like a benediction.

The Lexicon

Words, words, words.
Not a moment goes by
Without a conjunction or a clause.

You need coffee in the morning?
You coax and cajole the mix
To make the beverage hot and bitter.
Words make a stronger brew.

The dough of language.
Mix the salt of human life
And the leavening of hope,
And add many words.
Knead until as self-explanatory
As a baby's bottom.

Love is not silent.
We caress each other
With the lexicon of desire
And complication.
The climax? An ejaculation
Of words in celebration.

Wield the hammer in your hand;
You have a job to do.
There is no better measure
Than subject, verb, object.
The foundations are solid,
With the weight of grammar;
You line up the studs
With the perspicuity of poetry;
The windows are enjambed.
The roof is over-arching,
As all-encompassing as prose.

And then the words cease;
As life is logos, death is silence.
If you have used your words well
The silence is well deserved.
As every sentence must end,
Death puts a period to your periods.
May you rest in assurance
That your life has, indeed,
Been well stated.

On the Recollection of Safety

It is the scent of home.
The scramble home after school,
Scraped knees and bruised egos
Notwithstanding: the odor
Of safety, of solace, of family.

The process itself is calming:
The slurry of water, yeast, and sugar,
As sweet and fecund as young love.
Don't forget the salt: All human
Action is better with a grain of salt.
The batter thickens as you add flour;
As it matures, it becomes more resistant.
Finally, the dough forms: smooth and supple
As a baby's bottom or a woman's breast.
This is a human enterprise.

Through it all, however,
The sense of smell is supreme:
It eases me into the past.
The slab of bread in the morning,
The butter pooling on hot toast:
Sandwich bread that cannot
Be rolled into a ball and thrown;
The tussle over who gets
A piece of uncooked dough,
Soft, warm, infused with yeast;
And the soft inner piece
Where two loaves are baked together.

The senses, properly deployed,
Transcend themselves and create
A record of the ephemeral web,
A fabric of memory and love
That wraps our human lives.

Coffee Spoons

We don't measure out our lives
With coffee spoons;
It's more complicated.
The Great Human Impulse
To impose order on chaos,
On life itself.

Into every life some order
Might fall, or might not,
Generally by accident.
Like a Quattrocento apprentice,
We draw a grid to help us
Replicate perspective.
We start small and expand.
Each fork and plate properly placed;
The sheets drawn tight.
Our clothes are appropriately
Coordinated, our books in order,
Each car parked carefully
Within its personal white lines.
The jobs we do are perfect,
A manifestation of character.
Our mates are the complete
Complement to our aspirations.

Blake disliked the Ancient of Days,
With his insufferable measuring.
But how do his actions differ
From the sand circles we draw
To limn the scope of
Our transient lives?

The Fog

It is the fog I remember best.
Late at night I walk the main road.
There is no sidewalk: the town
Touts rural living, and sidewalks
Are just too suburban.
But it is suburban,
Row upon row of tract homes,
Station wagons, and bicycles,
The morning paper that, later,
I will deposit on their front porches.

The smoke of my Marlboro
Distinguishes itself from the fog,
A stinging counterpoint
To the damp solace of the air.
I am wearing a trench coat
That once belonged to a Marine
A head taller than I am.
I have no particular place to go.
The roadside, the cigarette, and me.
Nothing more or less.

My friends are all professors' spawn.
They have read all the best books,
They have traveled the world.
Their parents work in offices
Surrounded by books and papers;
My father conducts inventory
At the lumberyard where I stack
Rough redwood fence boards
In pickups, on flatbed trucks,
In station wagons with no kids in the back.

My friends are a beacon, an aspiration;
But my roots are middle class,
Embedded in suburbia without sidewalks,
In the fog and the cigarette smoke,
And the questions I think
I will answer when I'm 45.

But it is the fog I remember best:
A cloak or shroud, an envelope
Of anonymity; a protection
While I brood about those questions
That I will never answer in a long life.

Like Water

Life is like water;
It has no fixed form.
We swim against the current
Or float downstream.
No matter how we stroke it,
Our job is merely
To stay afloat.

Do we contradict ourselves?
Of course we do; or perhaps not.
It's not as if it were clear:
There are no answers
Of miraculous precision.
We try on a different role
In each context:
Tongue-tied and voluble,
Accommodating and recalcitrant,
Simple but complicated,
Smart but seriously confused,
Public but personally shy,
Loving but occasionally unkind.

Hey, you old dog: I know you, I think.
That compression of the lips
You designate a smile:
One of many veils
Behind which you hide.

Haibun for Love

The car windows were glazed with steam when we
ventured into new worlds, your skin on mine. As my
hand ran down your back, the gates opened, revealing a
valley of unexpected beauty. Every flowing stream tasted
of nectar, and the branches of the forest leaned down
to caress. In this verdant oasis could I wander forever.
Holding you, I fell asleep.

> That was long ago
> Before waking made such love
> Aspirational

What We Are Given

this is what I remember
in the early morning
life began as a gift from you
the sun your satellite
silence your language
in those moments
when the blood began to run
through the channels
of our waking bodies
there was no need
for hope or disappointment
because we were living
and that is all we are given

this is what I remember
that in the middle
of the hurly burly day
your presence stood against
the assaults of trivia
the necessity of the unnecessary
that you winnowed
whatever the moment demanded
to its elemental need
we were living
and that is all we are given

this is what I remember
that when the night fell
it was a benediction
and darkness was a balm
when night held us
a caress not a bond

the muteness of belief
desire and acceptance
a place where words
are unnecessary
where we were living
and that is all we are given

The Geologic of Love

If our love is tectonic,
Then let our masses collide:
We will raise mountains
And create valleys.
I will fall into your declivities.

Perseverance

I need to know the difference
Between perseverance and
Perseverance.

In one, I wear my yoke
And plow the furrows
Of my ideas, my hopes,
My regrets, contemplating
A rich harvest

As for the other:
Watch me bang my head
On the brick wall
Of failed expectations
Without loosening
One lamentable brick.

These Things are Real

The grip of a newborn's finger,
Fierce in anticipation of a life;
The cry of a child discovering
An insect's iridescent carapace;
The shock of biology,
The punch of first love;
The urgent need and release
Of honest desire;
A hand placed lightly on
A lover's belly as she sleeps;
The balm of your words
Soothing a person's heart;
Three notes played together,
The first, the third, the fifth;
The smell of cut wood
As your hand guides the saw;
The passage of time that teaches
Time is merely an illusion;
That moment when life ceases
And the soul breathes out.

Nothing can change these things:
Not the myth of money, or
The cacophony of want,
The momentary power of status,
The fawning of sycophants, or
The rejection of people
Who fail to see you as you are.

Ah, the distractions of human life.
What does not live within the body
Is but tawdry clothing on a stick.

The Saw

Those teeth: those wicked, sharp teeth.
They are bound to do my bidding,
To rend stout logs along the line
Of my pencil, my whim.
Teeth, how have I offended you
That you leap at the guiding hand
And waste your precision
On my malleable flesh?
Did you not see?
There was no line there.

The Love We Speak Of

the love we speak of
is not the love we feel

words draw strong lines
crayon boxes
dark and definitive walls
making dreams
clear and facile
and untrue
a festive Christmas
morning
colorful boxes
empty
as the family
wanders off
to contemplate
disappointment

there is something
between us
that heals
something that is unspoken
unaligned
silent and rich
the loam of being human
devoid of categories
like the roots
of the quaking aspen
our tremulous lives
are connected
giving us sustenance

because we are
a forest
bound
and nourished
by a single root

Father and Son

The home movie shows you
As you were in 1950:
Undershirt, clodhoppers,
Your khakis slung low.
You fought the good fight
Tending the bare yard
Of that tract house in Tracy.
Three of five children
Tangled between your legs
As you pumped the shovel
In the Central Valley loam.
That summer I was almost two.
My memory has nothing now
But that scratchy celluloid
And the aching, distant sensation
Of the heavy valley heat.

The cassette snaps into place
And I see myself on TV:
I extend my arms and balance
The child; each foot placed
Tentatively, he makes his way
Staggering among toys.
I pick him up and hold him,
Arms wrapped like smoke
Around a fire.
He pushes away and strikes me,
Unwilling to be obscured.

In the mirror this morning,
What is this shock of recognition?
I think of the child and then

I see your smile dance across
My lips. Strange double-take:
Your arm around me around the boy.
I feel your ready tears well up:
For me, for you, for the child
Whose pulsing movement
Slaps upon my face
The smile you wore for me.

On The Putting on of Power

My hand amazes me:
The resilience of the skin,
The work-hardened calluses,
The honest, broken nails.
Your gift to me when you died.
The essence of your legacy
Beats across my wrist
With fevered diligence:
Thus your power comes to me.

Your hand guides mine
As I guide the plane,
As I feel the smooth cut.
Your fingers laugh with mine
Dancing down the naked back
Of the woman I love.
If I have held a child
In play or pain or fear,
Your hand held mine,
Supporting my supporting hand.
And when my guitar sings
A chord sweet and inexplicable,
As much as mine your fingers
Have pressed the strings to wood.

So I stand erect, a man.
But I would drop from time to time
The mantle of your memory
To sit naked, child again,
Upon your sacred father's knee,
Cloaked in the gentle sinew
Of your living arms.

Clothed in Language

I have worked long hours
For you, my son,
Pounding the treadle
Of my tongue,
Weaving a stout cloth
Of subject, object, verb.
Its burrs and knots
Will scratch you:
The itch of language.

This is the family cloth.
In the violently blooming
Willamette Valley,
Your great great grandfather
Wrapped it around
His fractious family.
In Bogota, the Rozos,
The index finger jabbing,
The point made, hung
Their tapestry of language
For all to admire
Between the disputes and cups
Of steaming, sweet coffee.

It may be a sheet, a blanket;
A swaddling cloth or shroud;
A cloak of anonymity, or
A flag of recognition.
Make of it what you will,
Measure it to your own size.
And remember, too:
The roughest cloth, well worn,
Becomes translucent as silk.

Portrait of My Body

In the mirror, my body looks
Like an old friend.
The skin stretches across the muscle,
The arms balance, more or less.
Though the hair on my chest
Looks like a briar in winter,
It still grows under that mad snow.
The leather of my pate stretches
From chin to crown,
And glows with the rubbing of the sun.

The best of friends, too, may turn –
A conspiracy of corpuscles,
An insurrection of cells.
As surely as past lovers turn away,
Silently, my body shuns me,
Disgusted by necessary imperfection.

Naked I lean back upon
The crystal sphere of the earth.
I feel the sun's heat
Across my face, my chest,
The vulnerability of my belly,
The vast slabs of my thighs,
My penis – the fulcrum of all things –
My testicles. They absorb this heat
From outside, from afar.
My cells drink the sun instead of water,
They radiate that stolen light,
And I become transparent,
Like the earth upon which I lie.

Trochilidae

What is this jewel
clothed in the shimmering colors
of sea and grove, surge and leaf?

When the earth split
she graced you with
the blue of lightning
the orange of the angry sun
the green of seething jungle.

Autonomous, ferociously tiny,
unique among beating hearts,
the sound of your work,
the flash of your wings
humming, a contingent
of monks intoning
Om, meeting the embrace
of the universe.

O! mighty tiny one,
would that the trumpet vine
had not snared you!
You would have continued
with dagger focus
seeking the nectar
forbidden to the less stalwart,
filling our yard with
your life-affirming song.

Yet even death broadcasts
your splendor.
In your cloak of blue
and green and magenta,
you remain more alive than I.

Standard Time

It's that time again; that is,
The time when we play with time,
When we unfold the night
And tuck it around ourselves,
A dark consolation
When grim winter slouches in.

It's an odd game we play, imagining
We can roll the earth back an hour
Through the force of feeble humanness,
As if time and the earth cared.

In the Mojave, crystal cold
When the night falls,
In adjacent burrows
A rattlesnake and a ground squirrel
Wait out the winter.
They sense no change of time;
For them the world is physical.
On the California coast
A grove of redwoods stands
As it has for millennia,
Mute and irrevocable.
The Pacific fog on the needles
Gathers and then drops,
Like the ticking of a clock,
Saturating the ground cover.
For them, the sun rises when it rises
And sets when it is ready.
We play no role.

The Sierra Nevada, the backbone
Of this piece of earth,

Rises implacable to the east.
Mt. Whitney, Half Dome, El Capitan,
The granite vertebrae that hold us together.
They have known the sun and night
Since before humans concluded,
Mistakenly, they were masters
Of the universe. The mountains
Don't waste time on counting time.
When the night falls early,
Let us light a candle
We can call the sun.

Song of the Algorithm

Ah, the perfect life.
Everything
as smooth as glass.
0 1 0 1 0 1.

It is exhausting,
this fury and mire.
Reading a man's
face: anger or laughter?
Late at night
lying next to you,
so many questions.
Do you strike my hand
Away, playfully,
or with disgust?
The school yard voice
of children: Is it
the voice of God
or intruding cacophony?

The algorithm is
efficient,
eliminating
unnecessary
complications.
Your pain is yours,
not mine.
Over population?
Famine and war.
Too few workers?
You must procreate.
No need to waste time

imagining
the seething potential
of the school yard:
Those children await
the algorithm's
command.
Our touch in darkness:
a firing of neurons,
nothing more or less.

O! Algorithm, mi amor,
thou knowest
my desires,
and failings,
before I do.
0 1 0 1 0 1.
Like the beating
of my heart but
perfect.

Lack of Ars Poetica

of necessity
the poem writes itself
I sit daydreaming
and pay attention
to the sigh and crack
of the ranch house where we live
unknown people motoring past our house
the random rare smell
of the ground after rain
the lingering human presence
in the kitchen and bedroom
texture of the slick linoleum
the rough touch of brick

I am just here
the words, the images,
their presence climb
like ivy over my immobility
each leaf each tendril
sings a song of growth
and renewal, a song
that is not of me
like a tuning fork
I am just a medium
for the earth's vibration

Unnecessary Words

You will die, of course.
It happens as naturally
as conception, when
James slips through Janie's
window while
her parents are asleep.
At a certain point your face,
the image of a thousand
mid-western corn furrows,
will no longer be there for me.
Gone, those eyes that bestowed
love with a critique;
that smile containing
a generation of obduracy
you bequeathed to me.
I will miss you
as easily as peeling
the skin off my bones,
the bones you gave me,
that hold me up.

To Awaken

Do I ask too much
to face my mortality
with the understanding
of wild things?
We knew this once,
we lived
the life of prey,
we wandered
onto the savanna
cracking carrion bones
to suck out the marrow.
Knew this lush existence
persists for a moment
and then vanishes.

I would like to return
to the simple understanding,
so obvious, so clear,
That life dances
from the neurological brawl
of living
to the infinitude
of silence.

At the end
we awaken from living
with gratitude,
with our eyes wide open,
all questions
answered
or rendered moot,
all accomplishments
placed in perspective,
all reconsiderations
complete.

Acknowledgments

Special thanks to Les Bernstein and Amrita Skye Blaine, whose gentle insistence could coax poetry out of a rock.

Some of these poems have been aided and abetted by Redwood Writers (a branch of the California Writers Club), which has published the following poems:

"WTC" was published in *Phases* (Redwood Writers, 2023)

"Returning Favors" was published in *One Day* (Redwood Writers, 2024)

"Corduroy" was published in *One Day* (Redwood Writers, 2024)

"The Geologic of Love" was published in *The Smalls* (California Writers Club, 2025)

"Father and Son" was published in *Phases* (Redwood Writers, 2023)

"These Things are Real" was published in *Phases* (Redwood Writers, 2023)

Bios

Bart Scott is a lawyer living in Northern California, where he represents people accused, and sometimes guilty, of crimes. He has been writing since he was a kid, which was a while ago. He also plays guitar and sings, with mixed results. The author can be reached at *bartscottpoetry@sonic.net*

Lorna Ho is an artist working in Santa Rosa. She has a B.A. in Art History from the University of Hawaii and has honed her craft through numerous watercolor and collage classes at institutions and through private instruction. Her work has been featured in prominent exhibitions in Sonoma County, including the Santa Rosa Art Center, Sebastopol Center for the Arts, and the Healdsburg Center for the Arts. Lorna won second place in the Professional Division at the National Endowment for the Arts in 2022 and 2024, and Best of the Show at the 2023 Artists of Western Sonoma annual show.

9 7 9 8 9 9 2 3 0 2 3 7 0